Spotlight on
Kids Can Code

Understanding Coding Through

SIMULATIONS

Patricia Harris

PowerKiDS press™

New York

Published in 2017 by The Rosen Publishing Group, Inc.
29 East 21st Street, New York, NY 10010

First Edition

Editor: Caitie McAneney
Book Design: Michael J. Flynn

Photo Credits: Cover (boy) Susan Chiang/E+/Getty Images; cover, pp. 1, 3–24 (coding background) Lukas Rs/Shutterstock.com; p. 4 Uber Images/Shutterstock.com; p. 5 Nataliia Budianska/Shutterstock.com; p. 6 courtesy of Prussian Palaces and Gardens Foundation Berlin-Brandenburg; p. 7 Manchester Daily Express/SSPL/Getty Images; pp. 8–9 (character and screenshots) © Squad; p. 11 Jordan Tan/Shutterstock.com; p. 13 Visual Information Specialist Markus Rauchenberger/U.S. Army; p. 14 Joe Raedle/Getty Images; p. 15 https://en.wikipedia.org/wiki/Black_hole#/media/File:BH_LMC.png; p. 16 © Trivola; p. 17 Cora Mueller/Shutterstock.com; p. 19 John B. Carnett/Popular Science/Getty Images; p. 20 NASA/Paul E. Alers; p. 21 NASA/JPL-Caltech/MSSS.

Cataloging-in-Publication Data

Names: Harris, Patricia.
Title: Understanding coding through simulations / Patricia Harris.
Description: New York : PowerKids Press, 2017. | Series: Spotlight on kids can code| Includes index.
Identifiers: ISBN 9781499427943 (pbk.) | ISBN 9781499428223 (library bound) | ISBN 9781499428810 (6 pack)
Subjects: LCSH: Computer programming-Juvenile literature. | Computer simulation-Juvenile literature.
Classification: LCC QA76.52 H37 2017 | DDC 005.1-dc23

Manufactured in the United States of America

CPSIA Compliance Information: Batch #BW17PK: For Further Information contact Rosen Publishing, New York, New York at 1-800-237-9932

Contents

What Are Simulations?

Simulations help people understand large, **complex** problems using smaller, simpler **models**. The models represent the important parts of an event or process. Simulations show how those events or processes happen over time. Today, many important events and processes are the basis for computer simulations. However, not all simulations are on computers.

Computer programs allow us to create simulations that apply to real life. Simulations may be used to show weather patterns, construction plans, and medical procedures.

Some board games, such as Battleship, are simulations. There are two versions of Battleship—the old paper-and-pencil version and the board game with moveable pieces. In the paper-and-pencil version, two players fill in squares on grid paper to show where they want their ships to be located. The ships are represented by the squares they fill. Then, taking turns, each player names a square as a target by using its **coordinates**. This game is a simulation for war on the seas.

Kriegsspiel

In 1812, Georg Leopold von Reiswitz, a lieutenant in the Prussian Army, worked with his son to create a war game. He developed the simulation, called *kriegsspiel*, or "war game," to help train the army. It was a tabletop game with special pieces for changing the layout of the land, blocks for army units, dice, and specific rules. It even included what was known as the "fog of war." The fog was all the things the army leaders could not really know about a battle. The game master helped simulate the fog.

It wasn't an easy simulation to use. The officers in the Prussian Army found it very difficult. However, *kriegsspiel* is an important part of the history of simulations.

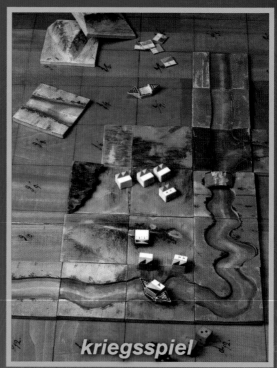

kriegsspiel

War games became very popular.
English author H. G. Wells created a
simple war game called Little Wars.

Computer Game Simulations

Like board games and war games, computer games may operate as simulations with models and changes. However, many of these game programs create places, characters, or powers that don't exist in reality. They ask the player to believe the unbelievable. Some games ask users to suspend their knowledge of the real world and embrace the new world of the simulation. This isn't just true in computer games. It's also true in some role-playing games based on written scripts or cards.

An example of a computer simulation that's fairly far from reality is the game *Spore*. Players raise a space-traveling alien life-form from a **spore**. *Kerbal Space Program* is a more recent game simulation with alien creatures. The creatures aren't real, but the space information behind the game is based on fact.

These are screenshots of the game *Kerbal Space Program*. The little green creature is an alien.

KERBIN
Info

A unique world, Kerbin has flat plains, soaring mountains and wide, blue oceans. Home to the Kerbals, it has just the right conditions to support a vast, seemingly undepletable population of the eager green creatures.

Reaching a stable orbit around Kerbin is one of the first things budding space programs strive for. It is said that he who can get his ship into orbit is halfway to anywhere

Simulations and Reality

It's amazing how computer simulations and reality are often very close. Flight simulators used to train pilots must be very close to reality. A system may even have an actual **cockpit** with all the normal controls.

A flight simulator for training pilots is more complex and expensive than anything you'll buy for home use. However, simulations that run on your home computer can still come quite close to reality. For example, the program. *Cities: Skylines* simulates the development of urban areas. Another program called *Farming Simulator* includes fields of various sizes and shapes to be planted and various crops to be harvested. The goal is to make the most money to pay for the equipment used for farming.

Breaking the Code

The equipment to support simulations can be as simple as a steering wheel for a driving program. Or they can be complex, such as the cabin of a space module used to train astronauts.

It's important for pilots to train on simulators before they actually start flying. That way they'll know what to do if an emergency arises.

Training Military and Police

You might be wondering why anyone would use computer simulations for training when they could use the real activity. Think about the military. Soldiers need to learn to use weapons before they're in an emergency situation. Otherwise they might risk injuring themselves or others and wasting expensive **ammunition**. This is a good time to use simulations.

Police also use computer simulations to train officers to better react to real-life situations. A simulation of an armed robbery allows officers to face this situation without injury to themselves or others. They can experience specific situations as well as the stress that comes with them. Some programs have a gun that interacts with the visual simulation. It's even possible to have the simulation include a device that delivers a shock if a **recruit** is shot.

Training new police recruits with computer programs is safer for the recruits and the people they serve. The programs use models and simulations to represent the reality of the situation.

Simulations in Different Fields

Computer simulations are used in many fields, including **meteorology**, physics, **astrophysics**, and social sciences. In many cases, they're used to help predict possible outcomes or events in the future.

In meteorology, scientists use simulations to track storms and try to understand what's happening in a weather pattern. Simulations are also used in physics research and education. A physics teaching simulation could show a boat crossing a river. The user can see what happens if the boat is pointed in different directions.

Simulations are very important when it comes to **forecasting** weather events, such as hurricanes and tornadoes. An accurate forecast can save lives.

black hole simulation

Astrophysicists use simulations to understand the growth of **black holes** in space. In social sciences, simulations are used to predict what might happen when one part of a social situation is changed. For example, a simulation might be used to predict what happens when a city changes its taxes over time.

Build Your World

Simulations in video games often involve real-world processes, such as driving a car. Some also include simulated social interactions. Games may require players to build or manage a community, often with a set amount of money and resources. The games may have players direct the lives of virtual people or animals, such as pets that exist only on the computer. Players may act as the caretaker for rescued pets, which simulates caring for an animal's real needs.

Some simulation games ask players to suspend their belief in reality. For example, players may have to care for strange beasts in a **fantasy** world. However, the caregiving tasks could echo the tasks of any caregiver in a real social setting. The player would still have to meet the beast's needs for food, water, and a clean environment.

Pet World 3D

Sometimes game simulations relate to common social situations. The program *Pet World 3D* allows players to clean cages, treat health problems, and find the animals new homes.

Building a Simulation

Building a computer simulation has two parts. The first part is knowing the reality on which the simulation is based. Reality has many components, or parts. These include the setting, changes over time, and physical features. If there's a human component, it could include what a person sees, hears, smells, and tastes. It could also include emotions, such as fear, anger, excitement, or confusion. Knowing the reality may take getting information from people who have experienced a situation or reviewing historical reports.

The second part is knowing what components are needed to lead a person through completing a task in the simulation. You might need special equipment to make the computer simulation more lifelike.

Breaking the Code

In order to create realistic training simulations, programmers need to understand the physical, sensory, and emotional components.

Creating a lifelike car-driving simulator requires several components. These include the visual simulations, as well as a steering wheel and pedals.

Garbage In, Garbage Out

There is an old **acronym** that applies to simulations: GIGO. It stands for "garbage in, garbage out." This means the quality of the data put into a program affects the quality of the results of that program.

NASA computer engineers and scientists test and retest all their work to assure the best quality data they can get. Data about Mars that comes directly from NASA could be used to make an accurate simulation about a trip to Mars.

Three types of data sources exist for simulations. One type of source is a **random** number generator. The second type of source is a program that uses data supplied by another program. If this data is from a reliable source, such as NASA, any simulation relying on it has less chance for "garbage out." The third source of input is data supplied by a person. The chance for "garbage out" is greatest with this type of input. Even typing errors can make for low-quality output.

Write Your Own Simulations

Writing code for simulations isn't easy, but it can be very fun and useful. A basic program for creating simulations is Insight Maker, which is a free-use online program. For example, with this program, you could create a simulation that answers the question: What happens to a rabbit population if no predators are present?

Whether you want to make a simulation to forecast weather events or to learn how to drive, coding is the key to predicting outcomes and building virtual realities.

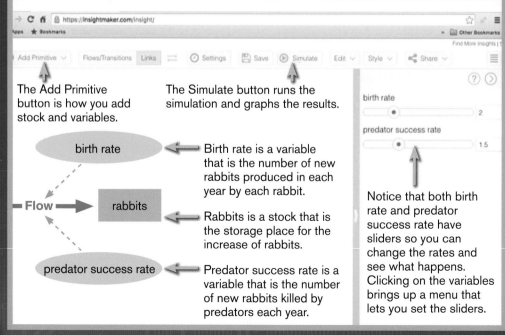

The Add Primitive button is how you add stock and variables.

The Simulate button runs the simulation and graphs the results.

birth rate   2

predator success rate   1.5

Birth rate is a variable that is the number of new rabbits produced in each year by each rabbit.

Rabbits is a stock that is the storage place for the increase of rabbits.

Predator success rate is a variable that is the number of new rabbits killed by predators each year.

Notice that both birth rate and predator success rate have sliders so you can change the rates and see what happens. Clicking on the variables brings up a menu that lets you set the sliders.

Glossary

acronym: A word formed from the first letters of each of the words in a phrase.

ammunition: Bullets, shells, and other things fired by weapons.

astrophysics: The science of the physical and chemical structures and properties of objects in outer space.

black hole: An invisible area in space with such strong gravity that light cannot escape it.

cockpit: The area in an airplane where the pilot sits.

complex: Having to do with something with many parts that work together.

coordinate: One of a set of numbers that's used to locate something on a graph, map, or other diagram.

fantasy: Something that is imagined and not real.

forecast: To make an informed guess about future weather.

meteorology: The scientific study of Earth's weather systems.

model: A smaller representation of something.

random: Chosen or done without a particular plan or pattern.

recruit: A new member of a military force.

spore: A small body made by a plant that can grow into another plant.

Index

Websites

Due to the changing nature of Internet links, PowerKids Press has developed an online list of websites related to the subject of this book. This site is updated regularly. Please use this link to access the list: www.powerkidslinks.com/kcc/simu